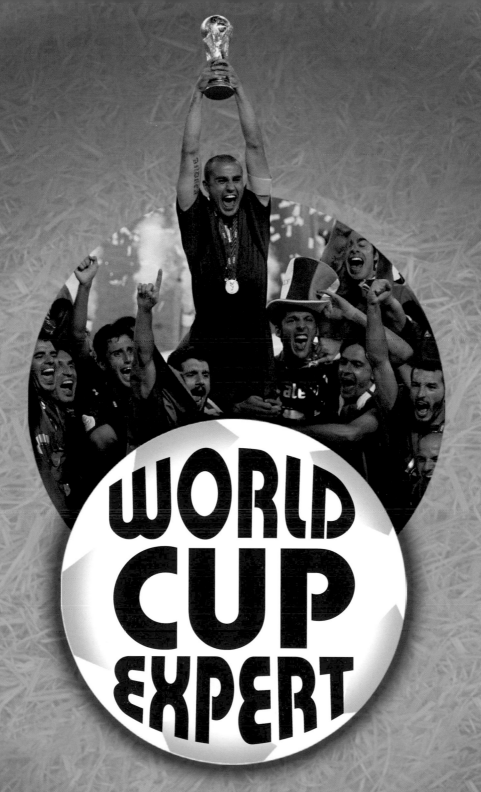

WORLD CUP EXPERT

TEAMS

Pete May

A+

Smart Apple Media

Published by Smart Apple Media, an imprint of Black Rabbit Books
P.O. Box 3263, Mankato, Minnesota 56002
www.blackrabbitbooks.com

Published by arrangement with the Watts Publishing Group, LTD, London.

Cataloging-in-Publication data is available upon
request from the Library of Congress
ISBN 978-1-62588-134-2

Series Editor: Julia Bird
Series Design: d-r-ink.com

Picture credits: AFP/Getty Images: 6, 16, 19c, 21. Allsport/Getty Images: 7b, 11b. The Asahi
Shimbun/Getty Images: 1, 23. Bongarts/Getty Images: 19b, 27t. Shaun Botterill/Getty Images:
27b. Gabriel Bouys/AFP/Getty Images: 25b. Philippe Caron/Sygma/Corbis: 20. Corbis Wire/
Corbis: 15. dpa/Corbis: 11t, 17. Fstockphoto/Shutterstock: 5t, 24. Getty Images: 5b. Keystone/
Hulton Archive/Getty Images: 10b. Michael King/Getty Images: 18. Andres Kudacki/Corbis: front
cover. Popperfoto/Getty Images: 8, 12,13. Christophe Simon/AFP/Getty Images: 25t. Philippe Le
Telier/Paris Match/Getty Images: 9b. Bob Thomas/Getty Images: 4r, 14, 22, 26.

987654321

CONTENTS

THE WORLD CUP

The World Cup is a month-long celebration of soccer which is held every four years. Teams from 32 countries battle it out on the field for the ultimate prize in soccer – the World Cup trophy.

WHAT MAKES A GREAT TEAM?

The World Cup tournament brings out the best in every team. Games are played at a high level of skill and often decided by a single goal in overtime. It is considered a great accomplishment to reach the championship game, even though only one team will take home the trophy.

BRAZIL, BRAZIL

In the history of the World Cup, there have been many excellent teams. In the past, Brazil has often been a dominant force and two of their teams are featured in this book. However, many countries have had memorable teams through the years.

CLASS ACTS

What qualities should a great team have? Sometimes it is simply world-class players and dramatic goals such as Brazil in 1958 and 1970, or possessing a genius who inspires their teammates, as was the case with Maradona's Argentina in 1986. Or it might lie in a quality team packed with talent such as France in 1998 or with a brilliant short-passing game such as Spain in 2010.

WORLD CUP FAST FACTS

FOUNDED: 1930

NUMBER OF TEAMS THAT TAKE PART: 32 (expanded from 16 in 1978 and again from 24 in 1982)

MOST SUCCESSFUL TEAM: Brazil

TOP GOAL-SCORER: Ronaldo (above) with 15

FORMAT: For the group stage, teams are put in eight groups of four teams. Each team plays all the other three teams once. The top two teams from each group qualify for the knock-out stages, where the winner of one group plays the runner-up of another. The winners of this qualify for the eight-team quarterfinals, which are followed by the semifinals and the long-awaited World Cup final itself.

Spain take on Honduras during a group match in the 2010 World Cup.

CHARACTER AND TEAM SPIRIT

But greatness can also lie in having the character to overcome adversity, as was the case with the Italy side of 2006. Memorable teams also possess the mental strength and determination to overcome obstacles and a supposedly better team, as West Germany proved by beating the Netherlands in 1974. In other cases, it might simply be that the team is a perfect fit and becomes more than the sum of its parts, as was the case with England in 1966.

Any selection of top ten World Cup teams will always be open to debate, and we hope that this book will inspire many discussions. But we hope you agree that these teams all deserve to be included.

England players celebrate a controversial goal against West Germany in the 1966 World Cup.

HUNGARY
1954

The Hungarian team line up for their national anthem.

FAST FACTS

UNIFORM: Red shirts, white shorts, white socks with red trim

MANAGER: Gusztáv Sebes

CAPTAIN: Ferenc Puskás

KEY PLAYER: Nándor Hidegkuti, the deep-lying centre forward

BEST PERFORMANCE: Thrashing the eventual winners West Germany 8–3 in a group game

Hungary's "Golden Team" of 1954 was one of the best team not to win a World Cup. A year earlier they had beaten England 6-3 at Wembley, in the so-called match of the century. The "Magical Magyars" were clear favorites to win the 1954 World Cup in Switzerland.

PLAYERS AND TACTICS

Under coach Gusztáv Sebes, the Magyars had a modern fitness program and tactics. Sebes played Nándor Hidegkuti as a deep-lying center-forward, a tactic that confused defenses. He introduced near-post crosses and an early version of "total soccer", with a short-passing game and players swapping positions. Central to the team was its striker and captain, the incredibly skillful Ferenc Puskás. Striker Sándor Kocsis was lethal in the air and on the ground. The side had a fine left winger in Zoltán Czibor and a world-class goalkeeper in Gyula Grosics.

TO THE FINAL

The Hungarians started the World Cup strongly, beating South Korea 9–0 with Kocsis scoring a hat-trick and Puskás scoring twice, then thrashing a weakened West Germany side 8–3. Unfortunately, Puskás received a hairline ankle fracture in the Germany match. Without their captain, the Hungarians showed their battling side by beating Brazil 4–2 in a fierce quarterfinal known as "the battle of Berne", with Kocsis scoring twice again in a game that saw three players ejected from the game. The semifinal was a classic. The Hungarians were two goals up against world champions Uruguay, before being pulled back to 2–2. In overtime, Kocsis scored with two great headers to propel his team into the final.

FIGHTING SPIRIT

All seemed to be going to plan in the final against West Germany. Puskás scored the first goal, playing through his injury. Zoltán Czibor put them 2–0 up after eight minutes. But they didn't count on a muddy field, some great saves by Toni Turek and the unbeatable spirit of the Germans, who tied the game. Hungary hit the post and bar and then, incredibly, West Germany scored a third goal through Rahn after 84 minutes. Even then, with two minutes left in the game, Puskás put the ball in the net, only to have the goal to be controversially disallowed for an offside call.

MEMORABLE MAGYARS

Before losing to West Germany, the Hungarians were unbeaten for 32 games and they scored 27 goals in the World Cup tournament. The West Germans staged one of the biggest upsets in World Cup history, but that Hungary team has never been forgotten.

DID YOU KNOW?

Ferenc Puskás was nicknamed "the Galloping Major". His first club team, Budapest Honvéd, was taken over by the Ministry of Defense and the players were given military ranks, so he really was Major Puskás.

Max Morlock of West Germany scores his team's first goal in the 1954 World Cup final.

Pelé brought new skill and flair to the World Cup.

BRAZIL 1958

FAST FACTS

UNIFORM: Yellow shirts with green trim, blue shorts, white socks with yellow and green trim.

MANAGER: Vicenta Feola

CAPTAIN: Hilderaldo Bellini

KEY PLAYER: Pelé, the 17-year-old boy who stunned the world with his skill and maturity

BEST PERFORMANCE: Scoring five goals in the final against Sweden, the host team

In 1958 the 17-year-old Pelé lit up the World Cup tournament. The world had seen nothing like the young genius from Brazil who scored a hat-trick in the semifinal and two goals in the World Cup final.

TALENTED TEAM

Manager Vicente Feola had an array of talent in his squad and also selected another youngster, Garrincha, a skillful right winger who had been born with deformed legs (his left leg curved outward and his right leg inward). He could fool defenders by twisting and turning in unusual directions. Vavá was a lethal striker, who also scored twice in the semifinal and final, while midfielder Didi was a great passer and free kick specialist.

TIME TO SHINE

In the group games Brazil beat Austria 3–0 and were held to a scoreless tie by England. Pelé was only selected for Brazil's final group game, a 2–0 win against the Soviet Union thanks to two Vavá goals, but then took the tournament by storm. In the quarterfinal Pelé scored the only goal against Wales, a chest trap and turn followed by a fine finish. In the semifinal he scored a sensational hat-trick as Brazil thrashed France 5–2.

FINAL GLORY

The final was a tense game for Brazil, playing the host team Sweden in front of a home crowd. Brazil was still haunted by the way their team had lost the 1950 World Cup final 2–1 at home to Uruguay, despite taking the lead. When Sweden scored after four minutes through Liedholm it looked like disaster might occur again. But Garrincha set up two goals for Vavá to put Brazil ahead at halftime. Then Pelé produced a brilliant third, flicking the ball over the head of a defender and turning to volley home. Zagallo added a fourth, before the Swedes managed to get one goal, but then Pelé scored a fifth goal on a header. The 17-year-old shed tears of joy at the final whistle before Brazil took their victory lap. This great Brazil team had won the World Cup for the first time and Pelé was on his way to becoming a global superstar.

DID YOU KNOW?

Garrincha also starred in the 1962 World Cup team and was one of the first soccer player to have a pop star girlfriend in samba singer, Elza Soares, whom he married in 1966.

Brazil celebrate winning the 1958 World Cup with a joyful victory lap.

ENGLAND
1966

"Some people are on the field... they think it's all over... it is now!" Geoff Hurst's fourth goal for England, accompanied by Kenneth Wolstenholme's commentary, provided English soccer with perhaps its greatest moment. Hurst scored a hat-trick as West Germany were beaten 4–2 in the 1966 World Cup final at Wembley.

FAST FACTS

UNIFORM: White shirts, navy blue shorts, white socks. Famously changed to second uniform of red shirts white shorts and red socks for the final

MANAGER: Sir Alf Ramsey

CAPTAIN: Bobby Moore

KEY PLAYER: Geoff Hurst, who replaced Jimmy Greaves and scored a hat-trick in the final

BEST PERFORMANCE: Recovering from the disappointment of a late tying goal from Germany to score twice in overtime in the final

NEW FORMATION
England won the World Cup through the tactical awareness of manager Sir Alf Ramsey. His team used a new 4-4-2 formation, relying on hard-working midfielders rather than wingers. England had world-class players in goalkeeper Gordon Banks, defender Bobby Moore and midfielder Bobby Charlton who was famed for his long-range shooting. Martin Peters was good at drifting into space and Alan Ball never stopped working.

GROWING CONFIDENCE
In the group matches England started nervously in a scoreless tie with Uruguay, but then defeated Mexico 2-0 with goals from Roger Hunt and a Bobby Charlton rocket. They went on to beat France 2-0 and defeated Argentina 1-0 in the quarterfinal after the Argentine captain Rattin was ejected from the game following a fierce clash on the field. In the semifinal, England beat Portugal 2-1. Stiles marked Portugal's star player Eusebio out of the game and Bobby Charlton scored twice, the second with a typically strong shot.

Sir Alf Ramsey

DISASTER STRIKES

Ramsey preferred the hard-working Hurst to crowd favorite Greaves in the World Cup final. Germany took the lead through Haller after just 12 minutes. But England tied the game through Hurst's header and then took the lead when Peters pounced on a rebound after 78 minutes. It looked like England's cup until two minutes from the end when Germany tied the game once more. As the players waited for overtime Ramsay showed his motivational skills, telling his men: "Look at the Germans, they're flat out... You've won the World Cup once, now go out and win it again."

TIME FOR HEROES

England responded. Hurst controlled the cross, turned and shot against the bar. The ball bounced on the goal line as Roger Hunt appealed for a goal. After consulting the linesman the referee confirmed the goal. It would have been a controversial winner, but in the final moments Moore remained the calmest man on the field as he shot a great long pass from defense to Hurst, who burst through the tired German defense to hammer the ball into the top of the net. England had won the World Cup for the first and only time.

Hurst heads home to equalize the game at 1–1.

DID YOU KNOW?

The World Cup trophy was stolen before the 1966 World Cup Finals. After seven days it was found in some south London bushes by a dog called Pickles.

England parades the World Cup in front of an ecstatic home crowd.

BRAZIL
1970

Brazil's 1970 World Cup winners were possibly the greatest team ever to play international soccer. This World Cup was the first to be shown on color TV and the dominant play of the Brazilians captivated audiences all over the world.

DID YOU KNOW?

Pelé is the only player to have three World Cup winners medals – for 1958, 1962 (he was awarded a medal later even though he was injured for the later games) and 1970.

Brazil's Tostão and Pelé celebrate a typically stylish Brazilian goal.

FAST FACTS

UNIFORM: Yellow shirts with green trim, blue shorts, white socks with green and yellow trim

MANAGER: Mário Zagallo

CAPTAIN: Carlos Alberto

KEY PLAYER: Gerson, whose passing orchestrated the dominant forward line

BEST PERFORMANCE: Demolishing Italy 4–1 in the World Cup final

The Brazilian and Italian teams line up before the 1970 final.

TEAM BRAZIL

Just as in 1958, the dynamic Pelé was the star of the team, scoring four goals during the tournament. However, manager Mario Zagallo could also call upon the explosive left-foot shooting of Rivelino and the skillful dribbling and finishing of Jairzinho, who scored in all six World Cup games. Striker Tostão was an able partner for Pelé up front, while midfielder Gerson was a great passer who set the pace of the team.

UPS AND DOWNS

Brazil's defensive lapses only added to the entertainment, as they beat Czechoslovakia 4–1 and Romania 3–2 in group games. Their game against England was a much tougher game, won 1–0 through Tostão's cross, Pelé's lay-off and Jairzinho's great finish. Peru was beaten 4–2 in the quarterfinal. In the semifinal, Brazil were a goal down to old rivals Uruguay but responded with a dramatic finish from Clodoaldo and late efforts from Jairzinho and Rivelino to win the game 3–1 and reach the World Cup final once again.

SAMBA GLORY

The final itself was a great display of attacking soccer against a defensive Italian side. Pelé scored a header to take Brazil ahead, only for a defensive lapse to let Boninsegna score a tie goal. Gerson scored the second goal with a thumping shot. Jairzinho poked home the third goal before captain Carlos Alberto overlapped to score possibly the greatest team goal in World Cup history. An eight-man passing move included midfielder Clodoaldo beating four men in his own half, and ended with Rivelino and Jairzinho setting up Pelé's pass and Alberto's superb drive into the bottom corner. The world could only sit back and admire the boys from Brazil.

NETHERLANDS 1974

Playing in gaudy orange shirts, the Netherlands team lit up the 1974 World Cup with "total soccer", a term invented by the Dutch media after the 4–1 demolition of Bulgaria in the group stage. Rinus Michels' team had players constantly changing positions, a new tactic which baffled the opposition.

FAST FACTS

UNIFORM: Orange shirts with black arm stripes, white shorts with orange stripes at sides, orange socks with black trim

MANAGER: Rinus Michels

CAPTAIN: Johan Cruyff

KEY PLAYER: Johan Cruyff, whose genius illuminated the World Cup

BEST PERFORMANCE: Beating Brazil 2–0 in the final group game

Johan Neeskens (left) and Johnny Rep of the Netherlands.

Neeskens sends the German goalkeeper the wrong way to score for the Netherlands.

TEAM EFFORT

Johan Cruyff was their star player, a superb dribbler, goal maker and playmaker. He gave his name to the "Cruyff turn", after a feint-and-drag back move that baffled that Sweden's right back Jan Olsson. Johan Neeskens was a skillful midfielder, while Johnny Rep was an exciting striker who scored four times. On defense, Arie Haan was a strong center back and Ruud Krol an attacking left back who could also score goals.

TOTALLY AMAZING

The genius of the Dutch team was evident in the second round as they defeated Argentina 4–0. Every goal was pure class; Cruyff's instant control as he rounded the keeper for the first, Krol's blast from the edge of the area, Cruyff's cross for a flying header and then Cruyff scoring from a seemingly impossible angle. A 2–0 victory over East Germany was followed by the crucial 2–0 defeat of a strong Brazil team in the semifinal. Neeskens scored with a dipping volley from Cruyff's cross. Then the Dutch produced a classic team goal, breaking from their own area with Krol's cross being met by Cruyff's flying volley. The Dutch had advanced to face West Germany in the World Cup final in Munich.

FINAL PAIN

If anything the Netherlands started the final too well, with a 14-man passing ending play, and an early goal. But they underestimated the German spirit and the support for the home team. Breitner tied the game with a disputed penalty and Gerd Müller grabbed a goal just before halftime. Despite several chances in the second half, the Dutch failed to score. But with their total soccer playing style, Adidas-sponsored uniform and cool sideburns, this Dutch team remains arguably the greatest team not to win the World Cup.

DID YOU KNOW?

While the rest of the Dutch team had three black stripes on their sleeves representing sponsor Adidas, Cruyff played with just two stripes as he was sponsored by rival Puma.

WEST GERMANY 1974

The West Germany team that won the World Cup in 1974 is often underrated simply because they beat the fan favorites, the Johan Cruyff-inspired Netherlands. But having the character to recover from an early setback proved the West Germans' heart and class.

West German defender Berti Vogts (right) tackles Australian forward Branko Buljevic during the group game between West Germany and Australia.

FINE FINISHERS

West Germany possessed a truly world-class striker in Gerd Müller. "Der Bomber" scored a total of 14 goals in the 1970 and 1974 World Cups. The team also had the great Franz Beckenbauer at the back, who excelled on both offense and defense. Wolfgang Overath was a fine playmaker and Sepp Maier a superb goalkeeper. In Paul Breitner they had an overlapping left back with a great shot who could confidently tuck away a World Cup penalty.

WINNING WAYS

West Germany beat Chile and Australia in their group matches. Ironically the only match they lost was a 1–0 defeat to East Germany. In the second round West Germany beat Yugoslavia 2–0, with a great 35-yard strike from Breitner and a grabbed goal from Müller. They scored four times in the second half against Sweden and, in a crucial last game on a soggy field, beat a fine Poland team 1–0 with a confident finish from Müller. Manager Helmut Schön

stood arms aloft on the sideline as the Germans reached the World Cup final.

AGAINST THE ODDS

In the final the Dutch scored with a penalty before any West German player had even touched the ball. It was a huge blow in front of a loud home crowd, but slowly the West Germans played themselves back into the game. Breitner scored a disputed penalty and the West Germans played their own brand of total soccer with defenders Beckenbauer and Vogts going close to scoring. Just before half-time Gerd Müller scored with a fantastic finish, somehow spinning to hook Bonhof's cross with the ball behind him. Sepp Maier had a great game in the second half as an inspired Berti Vogts' tough defensive play took Cruyff out of the game. The Dutch might have been in brilliant orange compared to West Germany's white and black, but the mental strength and superb skills of the West Germans deserved the ultimate prize.

West German players celebrate their second goal against the Netherlands.

FAST FACTS

UNIFORM: White shirts with black trim, black shorts, white socks

MANAGER: Helmut Schön

CAPTAIN: Franz Beckenbauer

KEY PLAYER: Gerd Müller might not have looked like a striker, but he had a great goal-scoring instinct

BEST PERFORMANCE: Overcoming the blow of an early penalty to beat the "total soccer" of the Dutch

ARGENTINA
1986

The phenomenal play of Diego Maradona meant fans often overlooked the contributions of his teammates in Argentina's 1986 World Cup victory.

SPIRITED TEAM

Defender José Luis Brown, who scored his only goal for Argentina in the World Cup final and then refused to be substituted despite having a dislocated shoulder, sums up the spirit of the team. Jorge Valdano was a fine attacking midfielder who scored four goals in the tournament, while Oscar Ruggeri was a talented defender. Though Maradona was unquestionably the star of the team, Argentina's manager Carlos Bilardo deserves much credit for his handling of Maradona, making him feel special by appointing him captain and building a team around his talents. Bilardo was rewarded by Maradona's inspired play.

BEST AND WORST

In the group stage, Argentina beat both South Korea and Bulgaria and 1-1 tied Italy thanks to Maradona's goal. In the quarterfinal against England, Maradona scored the infamous "Hand of God" goal with his hand, but then produced the "goal of the century", dribbling from his own half to beat five defenders and score. He then scored a sensational double in the semifinal win against Belgium.

Diego Maradona of Argentina in action during the 1986 World Cup.

FANTASTIC FINAL

The final against West Germany was a thriller. Despite Maradona being closely defended at every turn, Argentina went 2–0 up through Brown's header and Valdano's fine finish after 56 minutes. But West Germany once more showed all their fighting spirit to score twice and tie the game. Three minutes later, Maradona received the ball just inside his own half and found Jorge Burruchaga with a superb pass. The striker kept his nerve during a 40-yard run to slot the ball past Germany's Schumacher. Argentina held on, and ticker tape rained down from the stands as Maradona lifted the World Cup.

FAST FACTS

UNIFORM: Light blue and white striped shirts, black shorts, white socks

MANAGER: Carlos Bilardo

CAPTAIN: Maradona

KEY PLAYER: Maradona, who could turn a game around with one moment of genius

BEST PERFORMANCE: Beating West Germany 3–2 in the final having lost a two-goal lead

DID YOU KNOW?

Substitute Marcelo Trobbiani came on for the last two minutes of the final, equaling the record for the shortest ever World Cup career!

Burruchaga slides home Argentina's third and decisive goal.

FRANCE
1998

France's finest ever team was full of talent and character, and took France to World Cup glory for the first and only time in its history.

PACKED WITH TALENT

In goal was the dramatic Fabian Barthez, a great shot-stopper. The defense had excellent full-backs in Thuram and Lizarazu, the giant Marcel Desailly and the classy Laurent Blanc. Les Bleus had a solid midfield with the underrated Didier Deschamps shielding the defense, a number of creative players like Emmanuel Petit, Christian Karembeu and Youri Djorkaeff, and the genius of Zinedine Zidane supporting lone striker Guivarc'h.

GOLDEN GOALS

As the home team at the 1998 World Cup, France finally played to their potential. Manager Aimé Jacquet's men beat South Africa, Saudi Arabia and Denmark in the group stages with a young Thierry Henry scoring three times. France had to rely on an overtime "golden goal" (the first team to score in overtime won the match, a rule that was later dropped) from Laurent Blanc to defeat Paraguay in the knock-out match, before defeating Italy on penalties in the quarterfinals.

LATE DRAMA

The French showed character in the semifinal against Croatia, having fallen behind to a Davor Šuker goal.

Defender Lilian Thuram picked the perfect time to score his first ever international goal and then, amazingly, added a second, winning a tackle on the edge of the area and firing home with a perfect left-foot finish. Barthez made a crucial late tip-over save to advance the French team to the final. The match was marred by Croatia's Slaven Bilić going down after a clash with Blanc. Blanc was ejected from the game and missed the final through suspension.

WORLD CUP HISTORY

France met Brazil in the final at the Stade de France in Paris. Brazil's star striker Ronaldo had a seizure on the eve of the game, and although he did play, he was clearly not at his best. France took full advantage. Zinedine Zidane scored twice with powerful headers from corners to put France 2–0 up at halftime. Les Bleus survived Desailly being ejected after collecting a second yellow card, and in the 90th minute, substitute Patrick Vieira found his Arsenal teammate Emmanuel Petit, who scored a third goal to send France into ecstasy. The suspended Blanc joined in the celebrations as captain Didier Deschamps proudly lifted the World Cup trophy.

FAST FACTS

UNIFORM: Blue shirts with white arm stripes and red and white lines on chest, white shorts, red socks

MANAGER: Aimé Jacquet

CAPTAIN: Didier Deschamps

KEY PLAYER: Zinedine Zidane, who could find space anywhere on the field and scored twice in the World Cup final

BEST PERFORMANCE: Outplaying Brazil in the final and winning 3–0

French striker Thierry Henry takes the ball past Abdullah Zubromawi of Saudi Arabia.

France's players savor World Cup triumph at last.

DID YOU KNOW?

Goalkeeper Fabien Barthez insisted on a good luck kiss on his shaven head from teammate Lauren Blanc before every World Cup game.

ITALY 2006

The Italian team of 2006 proved its greatness through showing character in adversity. Following a corruption scandal in the Italian league, many of the Azzurri players were unsure of their future, and were not even sure if they would even be playing the following season.

FAST FACTS

UNIFORM: Blue shirts, blue shorts, blue socks

MANAGER: Marcello Lippi

CAPTAIN: Fabio Cannavaro

KEY PLAYER: Goalkeeper Gianluigi Buffon, who made a crucial save to deny Zidane the winning goal in the World Cup final

BEST PERFORMANCE: Beating Germany in the semifinal with two goals in the final two minutes of overtime.

DID YOU KNOW?

Ten different players scored for Italy in the tournament and five out of 12 goals were scored by substitutes, showing what a great team effort it was.

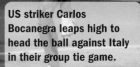
US striker Carlos Bocanegra leaps high to head the ball against Italy in their group tie game.

ENERGY AND RESOLVE

Goalkeeper Gianluigi Buffon had opted to stay with his team Juventus, relegated to the second division. He was outstanding in the World Cup, conceding just two goals. Center back and captain Cannavaro was one of the top players of the tournament. The energy of Gennaro Gatusso in midfield summed up the Italian spirit, while playmaker Andrea Pirlo provided the class. Italy had the best record in their group with two wins and a tie, but in the knockout stages had to wait for a 95th minute penalty to beat a plucky Australian team, before defeating Ukraine 3–0 in the quarterfinal, with Luca Toni scoring twice.

GREAT GAME

In the semifinal, Italy defeated an impressive German team 2–0 after overtime. It was a fast, exciting match. Buffon had already made a superb save from Podolski in overtime and as a penalty shoot-out loomed, the Italians scored twice in the final two minutes. After 119 minutes Fabio Grosso scored with a curling shot, having been found by a fine reverse pass from Pirlo. As Germany pressed, Cannavaro intercepted and

Italy captain and talisman Cannavaro proudly holds aloft the World Cup trophy.

found Gilardino who broke and rolled the ball to Del Piero, who scored with a left touch.

LATE DRAMA

In the World Cup final in Berlin, many expected veteran Zinedine Zidane to inspire France to victory. Zidane chipped in a penalty after seven minutes, but again the Italians refused to back down. Giant center back Materazzi tied the game after 19 minutes with a header and the final went into overtime. The critical moment came in the first period of overtime when Buffon produced a dramatic save to tip over Zidane's header. This seemed to unnerve Zidane so much that after an argument with Materazzi a few minutes later, he inexplicably headbutted him and was ejected from the game.

BRAVE BLUES

The game was tied at 1-1 at the end of regulation play, but Italy kept their nerve to win 5–3 on penalties. The deciding penalty was struck by Grosso, who was instantly tackled by his ecstatic teammates. The squad had every excuse to fail, but instead brought glory to the troubled world of Italian soccer.

Champions of the world – Spain rejoices in their World Cup success.

FAST FACTS

UNIFORM: Red shirts, blue shirts, red socks. Won the final in away uniform of all navy blue with red and gold stripes

MANAGER: Vicente Del Bosque

CAPTAIN: Iker Casillas

KEY PLAYER: Andrés Iniesta was at the heart of Spain's "tiki taka" system

BEST PERFORMANCE: Overcoming a resilient and skillful German side in the semifinal through Puyol's header

SPAIN 2010

This Spain team was renowned for its "tiki taka" short passing game. The heartbeat of the team was provided by Barcelona midfielders Andrés Iniesta and Xavi, who had exceptional playmaking skills.

BEST TEAM EVER?

Every player in Vicente Del Bosque's team was technically gifted, from center back Gerard Piqué to superb passer Xabi Alonso and brilliant finisher David Villa. The Spaniards had the experience of Iker Casillas in goal, Sergio Busquets holding the midfield, a classy right back in Sergio Ramos and a battle-hardened defender in rugged Carlos Puyol. Players as gifted as David Silva, Cesc Fabregas and Fernando Torres could not even get into the starting eleven.

GETTING THROUGH

Spain might not have won any tournament games by a large margin, but they always did enough to win, overcoming a shocking first-game defeat to Switzerland. Portugal was beaten by a David Villa goal in the knock-out match, while in the quarterfinal against Paraguay both teams had a penalty saved before Villa again gave Spain the win with his fifth goal of the tournament. The mark of a great team is that they can win games through unexpected means. Spain did

that against Germany in the semifinal, scoring an unusually direct goal as Puyol rose to meet Xavi's corner and thump a header into the net.

FIERY FINALE

The final against the Netherlands in Johannesburg was fierce battle, full of strong tackles and with few opportunities to score. Dutch defender Heitinga was ejected in overtime and the game was scoreless until Jesus Navas burst into the Dutch half and started a play that resulted in the ball rebounding off a defender to Fabregas. He found Iniesta with a short pass and the little midfielder drove the bouncing ball into the corner of the net. The goal sparked delirium as Iniesta ran to the corner and took off his jersey to reveal a white vest with a tribute to the late Dani Jarque, a former youth soccer player who died in 2009. The Spanish teammates crowded around Iniesta in jubilation. That moment showed the togetherness of the Spain squad as a nation rejoiced at winning its first World Cup trophy.

DID YOU KNOW?

Iker Casillas became the third goalkeeping captain to lift the World Cup, following the example of two Italians, Gianpiero Combi in 1934 and Dino Zoff in 1982.

Rugged Spanish defender Carlos Puyol heads the only goal of the game in the 2010 World Cup semifinal against Germany.

AGAINST THE ODDS

Here are a few teams that have produced some of the World Cup's biggest upsets...

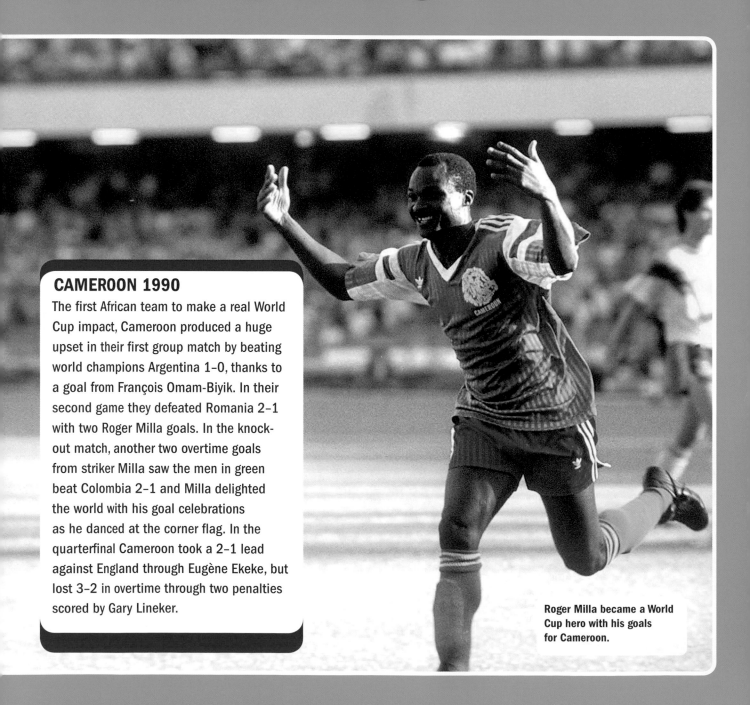

CAMEROON 1990

The first African team to make a real World Cup impact, Cameroon produced a huge upset in their first group match by beating world champions Argentina 1–0, thanks to a goal from François Omam-Biyik. In their second game they defeated Romania 2–1 with two Roger Milla goals. In the knock-out match, another two overtime goals from striker Milla saw the men in green beat Colombia 2–1 and Milla delighted the world with his goal celebrations as he danced at the corner flag. In the quarterfinal Cameroon took a 2–1 lead against England through Eugène Ekeke, but lost 3–2 in overtime through two penalties scored by Gary Lineker.

Roger Milla became a World Cup hero with his goals for Cameroon.

Croatia's first ever World Cup campaign was exciting and memorable.

CROATIA 1998

Only recognized as a country in 1992 following the Croatian War of Independence, Croatia finished third in the 1998 World Cup. This team boasted fine players such as Davor Šuker, Igor Štimac, Slaven Bilić, Robert Jarni, Zvonimir Boban and Mario Stanić. They beat Romania in the knock-out round, but the highlight of the tournament came with a 3–0 quarterfinal thrashing of Germany with goals from Jarni, Vlaović and Šuker. Croatia took the lead in the semifinal through a typically fine finish from Šuker, but were beaten by two goals from France's Thuram. In the third-place match Croatia defeated a strong Netherlands team 2–1.

SOUTH KOREA 2002

South Korea proved Asian soccer was on the rise by reaching the World Cup semifinal in 2006. Cleverly organized by Russian manager Gus Hiddink, the team was inspired by vocal support from its red-shirted fans. In the knock-out round Italy took the lead, but South Korea tied up the game just before the end of regulation play. In overtime Ahn Jung-Hwan scored the golden goal that sent the home crowd into ecstasy. Even more excitement was to follow, with the Koreans defeating Spain 5–3 on penalties in the quarterfinal to become the first Asian team ever to reach the semifinals. The team fought hard in the semifinal against Germany, but were ultimately beaten by Michael Ballack's late goal.

South Korea's players celebrate reaching the World Cup semifinal – the first time an Asian team has achieved this.

WORLD CUP

1. **Who scored the winning goal in the 1974 World Cup final?**
   a) Johan Cruyff
   b) Gerd Müller
   c) Paul Breitner

2. **Who was the captain of England who received the World Cup trophy in 1966?**
   a) Bobby Charlton
   b) Geoff Hurst
   c) Bobby Moore

3. **What was the nickname of Hungary's 1954 star Ferenc Puskás?**
   a) The Galloping Major
   b) The Striking Sergeant
   c) The Midfield General

4. **What did Andrés Iniesta do after scoring the winning goal for Spain in the 2010 World Cup final?**
   a) Remove his shirt
   b) Kiss the turf
   c) Perform a double somersault

5. **Who was the Italian player head-butted in the chest by Zinedine Zidane in the 2006 World Cup final?**
   a) Andrea Pirlo
   b) Gianluigi Buffon
   c) Marco Materazzi

6. **Who was the manager of England's 1966 World Cup winning team?**
   a) Bobby Robson
   b) Walter Winterbottom
   c) Alf Ramsey

7. **How did Diego Maradona score his first goal against England in the 1986 World Cup?**
   a) Hand of God
   b) Head of Diego
   c) Knee of Argentina

8. **What was the name of Spain's passing style at the 2010 World Cup?**
   a) Ticker tape
   b) Tick tock
   c) Tiki taka

9. **Who scored Brazil's fourth goal in the 1970 World Cup Final, often said to be the greatest team goal of any World Cup?**
   a) Pelé
   b) Carlos Alberto
   c) Jairzinho

10. **What team did Italy beat with two goals in two minutes of the semifinal of the 2006 World Cup?**
    a) Brazil
    b) Spain
    c) Germany

11. **What term referred to the Netherlands' style of play at the 1974 World Cup?**
    a) Total insanity
    b) Total soccer
    c) Total chaos

EXPERT QUIZ

12. Who scored France's third goal in the 1998 World Cup final victory against Brazil?
a) Zinedine Zidane
b) Marcel Desailly
c) Emmanuel Petit

13. Who was the goalkeeper captain who lifted the 2010 World Cup for Spain?
a) Iker Casillas
b) Victor Valdes
c) Pepe Reina

14. What team did Pelé score a hat-trick against in the 1958 World Cup semifinal?
a) France
b) Sweden
c) West Germany

15. Geoff Hurst scored a hat-trick in the 1966 World Cup Final for England. But who scored England's other goal?
a) Alan Ball
b) Bobby Charlton
c) Martin Peters

16. The 1974 Netherlands team played in what color shirts?
a) Gold
b) Orange
c) Yellow

17. Where in South Africa was the 2010 World Cup final played?
a) Johannesburg
b) Cape Town
c) Durban

18. In the 1954 World Cup, Hungary lost to West Germany 3–2 in the final, but had earlier beaten them in the group stages. By what score did Hungary win?
a) 5–3
b) 8–3
c) 6–2

19. Who was captain of West Germany's victorious 1974 team?
a) Franz Beckenbauer
b) Sepp Maier
c) Berti Vogts

20. Which Brazil player scored in every game of the 1970 World Cup?
a) Pelé
b) Rivelino
c) Jairzinho

Answers: 1)b 2)c 3)a 4)a 5)c 6)c 7)a 8)c 9)b 10)c 11)b 12)c 13)a 14)a 15)c 16)b 17)a 18)b 19)a 20)c

GLOSSARY

4-4-2 formation: A soccer team formation made up of four defenders, four midfielders and two strikers

Adversity: Hardship. A difficult period of time when things are not going well for a team

Center forward: The main striker, often a bigger player in the middle of the front line

Character: Teams are said to show character when they overcome a series of setbacks to gain something from a game

Chest trap: Controlling the ball on your chest

Concede: To let in a goal

Cruyff turn: A move made popular by Johan Cruyff in 1974. It involves a dummy-and-drag back of the ball that deceives a defender.

Free kick: Awarded when a player is fouled. The fouled team is given a free kick at the ball with no opposition player allowed within ten yards (9.1 meters) of them.

Golden goal: A rule, later abandoned, where the first team to score in overtime then wins the match.

Handball: When a player controls the ball with his hand

Hat-trick: When a player scores three goals.

Injury-time: The time added to a game by the referee after the standard 90 minutes are finished

Lap of honor: When the winning team run around the field to celebrate a win with their fans

Overtime: A period of 30 extra minutes that is played if a knock-out game is tied at the end of regulation play.

Playmaker: A midfield player who can create scoring opportunities against a defense through the use of clever passes and dribbling skill

Relegate: To go down a level or division

Samba soccer: Samba is a type of music and dance that is popular in Brazil. Samba soccerl describes the skillful, joyful style of Brazilian soccer.

Shot-stopper: A goalkeeper capable of fine saves is referred to as a shot-stopper

Tactics: The formations and changes of player that managers use to try to win games

Tiki taka: The short-passing style of play made famous by the Spanish soccer team

Total soccer: A fluid style of play created by the Netherlands team of 1974 involving players skillful enough to swap positions

WORLD CUP WINNERS

Year	Winners	Final score	Runners-up	Venue	Location
1930	Uruguay	4-2	Argentina	Estadio Centenario	Montevideo, Uruguay
1934	Italy	2-1	Czechoslovakia	Stadio Nazionale PNF	Rome, Italy
1938	Italy	4-2	Hungary	Stade Olympique de Colombes	Paris, France
1950	Uruguay	2-1	Brazil	Estádio do Maracanã	Rio de Janeiro, Brazil
1954	West Germany	3-2	Hungary	Wankdorf Stadium	Bern, Switzerland
1958	Brazil	5-2	Sweden	Råsunda Stadium	Solna, Sweden
1962	Brazil	3-1	Czechoslovakia	Estadio Nacional	Santiago, Chile
1966	England	4-2	West Germany	Wembley Stadium	London, England
1970	Brazil	4-1	Italy	Estadio Azteca	Mexico City, Mexico
1974	West Germany	2-1	Netherlands	Olympiastadio	Munich, West Germany
1978	Argentina	3-1	Netherlands	Estadio Monumental	Buenos Aires, Argentina
1982	Italy	3-1	West Germany	Santiago Bernabéu	Madrid, Spain
1986	Argentina	3-2	West Germany	Estadio Azteca	Mexico City, Mexico
1990	West Germany	1-0	Argentina	Stadio Olimpico	Rome, Italy
1994	Brazil	3-2*	Italy	Rose Bowl	Pasadena, California, USA
			(*All goals scored on penalty kicks; score was 0-0 after regulation play)		
1998	France	3-0	Brazil	Stade de France	Paris, France
2002	Brazil	2-0	Germany	International Stadium	Yokohama, Japan
2006	Italy	1-1	France	Olympiastadion	Berlin, Germany
2010	Spain	1-0	Netherlands	Soccer City	Johannesburg, South Africa

FURTHER INFORMATION

WEB LINKS

www.sportillustrated.cnn.com/soccer/news
World Cup 2014 Outlook

www.fifa.com/worldcup/index.html
The official website of the World Cup

news.bbc.co.uk/sport1/hi/football/world_cup_2010/8808966.stm
Iniesta wins the World Cup for Spain (2010)

www.youtube.com/watch?v=U1k7DGqRF5g
The famous Cruyff turn (1974)

BOOKS

U.S. Men's National Soccer Team: Looking up to 2014 FIFA World Cup, (Create Space, 2012)

Foul Football: Wicked World Cup, Michael Coleman (Scholastic, 2010)

The World Cup: World Cup 2010, Michael Hurley (Heinemann, 2010)

INDEX